W9-BET-769

Maritime
Colours

a book of colours from Canada

written and illustrated by

J.R.Mason-Browne

FOUR
EAST
PUBLICATIONS

Colours,
colours
all around...

A brown dog lives
in Charlottetown.

Purple clams cluster
on a Lunenburg beach.

On the chimney tops
high above North Sydney
a black crow caws.

On the road to Green Gables
a girl with red hair
meets a red fox.

In St. Andrews by-the-Sea

an orange cat sat.

Funny grey seals
leap and frolic
in the Northumberland Strait.

A duck
dives
deep
down
into Peggy's Cove
and finds a   pink   crab.

Behind the houses in Halifax
a white rabbit hops.

Near Fredericton yellow chicks peck between the sticks.

A green frog leaps
in Cavendish.

A blue jay
flies home
to Mahone Bay.

Wow!
Colours, colours

everywhere in the Maritimes!

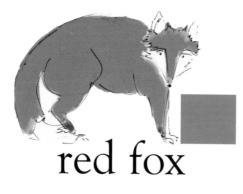

red fox

green frog

blue jay

purple clam

yellow chick

orange cat

white rabbit

brown dog

black crow

pink crab

grey seal

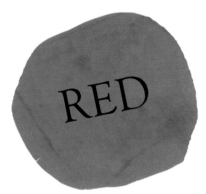

RED

These colours are used
to make every
other colour.

YELLOW

Blue

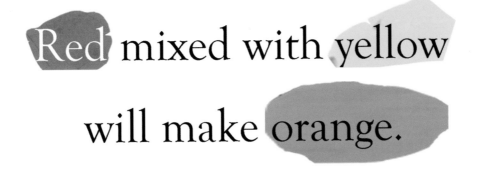

Red mixed with yellow

will make orange.

Yellow mixed with blue

will make green.

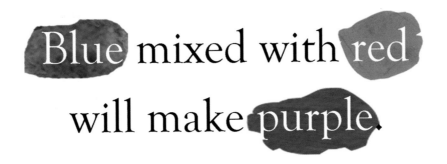

Blue mixed with red

will make purple.

For Rosemary and Neville

Copyright ©2014 J.R. Mason-Browne
All rights reserved.
First printing August 1, 2014
Except for the quotation of short passages for review purposes,
no part of this publication may be reproduced in any form without the permission of the author.

editing by Grayce Rogers
text and cover layout and design by J.R. Mason-Browne
Printed and bound in Canada
This is a work of fiction.
Any resemblance to actual events or persons, living or dead, is purely coincidental.
Published in Canada by Four East Publications
P.O. Box 3087 Tantallon, Nova Scotia B3Z 4G9
www.glenmargaret.com
Library and Archives of Canada Cataloguing in Publication
Mason-Browne, Jane, 1958-, author
Maritime colours : a book of colours from Canada / J.R. Mason-Browne
ISBN 978-1-897462-32-4 (pbk.)
1. Maritime Provinces~Description and travel~Juvenile literature.
2. Maritime Provinces~Pictorial works~Juvenile literature. I. Title.
FC2025.6.M37 2014   j971.5   C2014-906015-7